FRANCIS FRITH'S

GRANGE-OVER-SANDS

PHOTOGRAPHIC MEMORIES

ROBERT SWAIN was born in Lancashire at Cleveleys, near Blackpool. Whilst still a schoolboy he moved near to Lancaster, and he has lived there for over fifty years - he feels he is now becoming a local. He has a deep love of Lancashire, including the Over Sands area (which is now in Cumbria for administrative purposes). Robert is regularly to be seen out with his dog walking somewhere in the Lancashire countryside; he often walks on the bank of the Lancaster Canal, and has written a book on the subject. Robert has also written 'The Furness and Cartmel Peninsulas' for The Francis Frith Collection.

FRANCIS FRITH'S
PHOTOGRAPHIC MEMORIES

GRANGE-OVER-SANDS

PHOTOGRAPHIC MEMORIES

ROBERT SWAIN

First published in the United Kingdom in 2005 by The Francis
Frith Collection®

Hardback edition published in 2005 ISBN 1-84589-007-8

Paperback edition 2005 ISBN 1-85937-801-3

British Library Cataloguing in Publication Data

Grange Over Sands - Photographic Memories
Robert Swain

The Francis Frith Collection
Frith's Barn, Teffont,
Salisbury, Wiltshire SP3 5QP
Tel: +44 (0) 1722 716 376
Email: info@francisfrith.co.uk
www.francisfrith.co.uk

Printed and bound in Great Britain

Front Cover: **GRANGE-OVER-SANDS**, *The Pier 1914* 67426t
Frontispiece: **GRANGE-OVER-SANDS**, *Main Street c1955* G42087

*The colour-tinting is for illustrative purposes only, and is not intended to be
historically accurate*

Aerial photographs reproduced under licence from
Simmons Aerofilms Limited.
Historical Ordnance Survey maps reproduced under licence from
Homecheck.co.uk

Every attempt has been made to contact copyright holders of
illustrative material. We will be happy to give full acknowledgement in
future editions for any items not credited. Any information should be
directed to The Francis Frith Collection.

AS WITH ANY HISTORICAL DATABASE THE FRITH ARCHIVE IS
CONSTANTLY BEING CORRECTED AND IMPROVED AND THE
PUBLISHERS WOULD WELCOME INFORMATION ON OMISSIONS
OR INACCURACIES

CONTENTS

FRANCIS FRITH
VICTORIAN PIONEER

FRANCIS FRITH, founder of the world-famous photographic archive, was a complex and multi-talented man. A devout Quaker and a highly successful Victorian businessman, he was philosophical by nature and pioneering in outlook.

By 1855 he had already established a wholesale grocery business in Liverpool, and sold it for the astonishing sum of £200,000, which is the equivalent today of over £15,000,000. Now a very rich man, he was able to indulge his passion for travel. As a child he had pored over travel books written by early explorers, and his fancy and imagination had been stirred by family holidays to the sublime mountain regions of Wales and Scotland. 'What lands of spirit-stirring and enriching scenes and places!' he had written. He was to return to these scenes of grandeur in later years to 'recapture the thousands of vivid and tender memories', but with a different purpose. Now in his thirties, and captivated by the new science of photography, Frith set out on a series of pioneering journeys up the Nile and

to the Near East that occupied him from 1856 until 1860.

INTRIGUE AND EXPLORATION

These far-flung journeys were packed with intrigue and adventure. In his life story, written when he was sixty-three, Frith tells of being held captive by bandits, and of fighting 'an awful midnight battle to the very point of surrender with a deadly pack of hungry, wild dogs'. Wearing flowing Arab costume, Frith arrived at Akaba by camel sixty years before Lawrence of Arabia, where he encountered 'desert princes and rival sheikhs, blazing with jewel-hilted swords'.

He was the first photographer to venture beyond the sixth cataract of the Nile. Africa was still the mysterious 'Dark Continent', and Stanley and Livingstone's historic meeting was a decade into the future. The conditions for picture taking confound belief. He laboured for hours in his wicker dark-room in the sweltering heat of the desert, while the volatile chemicals fizzed dangerously in their trays. Back in London he exhibited his photographs and was 'rapturously cheered' by members of the Royal Society. His reputation as a photographer was made overnight.

VENTURE OF A LIFE-TIME

Characteristically, Frith quickly spotted the opportunity to create a new business as a specialist publisher of photographs. He lived in an era of immense and sometimes violent change.

For the poor in the early part of Victoria's reign work was exhausting and the hours long, and people had precious little free time to enjoy themselves. Most had no transport other than a cart or gig at their disposal, and rarely travelled far beyond the boundaries of their own town or village. However, by the 1870s the railways had threaded their way across the country, and Bank Holidays and half-day Saturdays had been made obligatory by Act of Parliament. All of a sudden the working man and his family were able to enjoy days out and see a little more of the world.

With typical business acumen, Francis Frith foresaw that these new tourists would enjoy having souvenirs to commemorate their days out. In 1860 he married Mary Ann Rosling and set out on a new career: his aim was to photograph every city, town and village in Britain. For the next thirty years he travelled the country by train and by pony and trap, producing fine photographs of seaside resorts and beauty spots that were keenly bought by millions of Victorians. These prints were painstakingly pasted into family albums and pored over during the dark nights of winter, rekindling precious memories of summer excursions.

THE RISE OF FRITH & CO

Frith's studio was soon supplying retail shops all over the country. To meet the demand he gathered about him a small team of photographers, and published the work of independent artist-photographers of the calibre of Roger Fenton and Francis Bedford. In order to gain some understanding of the scale of Frith's business one only has to look at the catalogue issued by Frith & Co in 1886: it runs to some 670 pages, listing not only many thousands of views of the British Isles but also many photographs of most European countries, and China, Japan, the USA and Canada - note the sample page shown on page 9 from the hand-written Frith & Co ledgers recording the pictures. By 1890 Frith had created the greatest specialist photographic publishing company in the world, with over 2,000 sales outlets - more than the combined number that Boots and WH Smith have today! The picture on the next page shows the Frith & Co display board at Ingleton in the Yorkshire Dales (left of window). Beautifully constructed with a mahogany frame and gilt inserts, it could display up to a dozen local scenes.

POSTCARD BONANZA

The ever-popular holiday postcard we know today took many years to develop. In 1870 the Post Office issued the first plain cards, with a pre-printed stamp on one face. In 1894 they allowed other publishers' cards to be sent through the mail with an attached adhesive halfpenny stamp. Demand grew rapidly, and in 1895 a new size of postcard was permitted called the court card, but there was little room for illustration. In 1899, a year after Frith's death, a new card measuring 5.5 x 3.5 inches became the standard format, but it was not until 1902 that the divided back came into being, so that the address and message could be on one face and a full-size illustration on the other. Frith & Co were in the vanguard of postcard development: Frith's sons Eustace and Cyril continued their father's monumental task, expanding the number of views offered to the public and recording more and more places

At the top left is a handwritten ledger/list with entries including:

St Catherine's College
Senate House & Library
Gerrard Hostel Bridge
Geological Museum
Addenbrooke's Hospital
St Mary's Church
Fitzwilliam Museum, Pitt Press &c
Buxton, The Crescent
The Colonnade
Public Gardens
Haddon Hall, View from the Terrace
Miller's Dale

in Britain, as the coasts and countryside were opened up to mass travel.

Francis Frith had died in 1898 at his villa in Cannes, his great project still growing. The archive he created continued in business for another seventy years. By 1970 it contained over a third of a million pictures showing 7,000 British towns and villages.

FRANCIS FRITH'S LEGACY

Frith's legacy to us today is of immense significance and value, for the magnificent archive of evocative photographs he created provides a unique record of change in the cities, towns and villages throughout Britain over a century and more. Frith and his fellow studio photographers revisited locations many times down the years to update their views, compiling for us an enthralling and colourful pageant of British life and character.

We are fortunate that Frith was dedicated to recording the minutiae of everyday life, for it is this sheer wealth of visual data, the painstaking chronicle of changes in dress, transport, street layouts, buildings, housing, engineering and landscape that captivates us so much today. His remarkable images offer us a powerful link with the past and with the lives of our ancestors.

THE VALUE OF THE ARCHIVE TODAY

Computers have now made it possible for Frith's many thousands of images to be accessed almost instantly. Frith's images are increasingly used as visual resources, by social historians, by researchers into genealogy and ancestry, by architects and town planners, and by teachers involved in local history projects.

In addition, the archive offers every one of us an opportunity to examine the places where we and our families have lived and worked down the years. Highly successful in Frith's own era, the archive is now, a century and more on, entering a new phase of popularity. Historians consider the Francis Frith Collection to be of prime national importance. It is the only archive of its kind remaining in private ownership. Francis Frith's archive is now housed in an historic timber barn in the beautiful village of Teffont in Wiltshire. Its founder would not recognize the archive office as it is today. In place of the many thousands of dusty boxes containing glass plate negatives and an all-pervading odour of photographic chemicals, there are now ranks of computer screens. He would be amazed to watch his images travelling round the world at unimaginable speeds through internet lines.

The archive's future is both bright and exciting. Francis Frith, with his unshakeable belief in making photographs available to the greatest number of people, would undoubtedly approve of what is being done today with his lifetime's work. His photographs depicting our shared past are now bringing pleasure and enlightenment to millions around the world a century and more after his death.

GRANGE-OVER-SANDS
AN INTRODUCTION

ABOUT 350 MILLION years ago, Grange-over-Sands and the surrounding area lay under a warm tropical sea, where the limestone rock of the area was formed. Later, Grange was covered by ice during the ice ages. It gets its name from a grange (or farm) in the area owned by the monks of Cartmel Priory (the word is derived from the French for 'barn' or 'granary'); 'over-Sands' was added later to distinguish it from places such as Grange-in-Borrowdale. Its neighbouring settlements are much older, and it is probably best to look at them first.

King Ecgfrith of Northumbria gave the land of Cartmel and all the Britons in it to St Cuthbert sometime between AD 670 and AD 685. It is probable that the local place of worship about that time was Kirkhead, near Allithwaite. The priory was founded by William Marshall, who later became the Earl of Pembroke, between 1190 and 1196, after his marriage to the very wealthy heiress Isabel de Clare. Unfortunately, all the archives and cartulary of Cartmel Priory have been lost, so that there is no record of its possessions.

The priory was built over a number of years. It is noticeable when studying the interior how

elaborate the oldest work is - no expense was spared. The monks of Cartmel wore black habits, because it was an Augustinian foundation; the priory was never to become as wealthy as Furness Abbey. The monks did not have as strict a rule of silence, and were allowed to eat meat at times. The priory was never raised to abbey status; it had to have an altar for the local people, which was in the south part of the church. This was the reason for Cartmel being spared at the Dissolution of the Monasteries in the 1530s, as Furness Abbey was. When the royal officials arrived to suppress the priory, they had to ask their superiors: 'Item, for the parish church of Cartmel, whether it stand unplucked down or no'. The reply was: 'Ordered by Mr Chancellor of the Duchy (of Lancaster) that it stand still'. As a result, we still have the priory today.

It is a matter of debate as to how much damage was done to the roof above the choir at the Reformation. However, the seats and benches, which date from about 1430 to 1440, were preserved, and only one of the misericords has been lost. Each of them has a different main design: some are carved with the heads of real or imaginary beasts, others have foliar designs, and there are a few other subjects. Small carvings, mainly of foliage, flank these designs. Work on the restoration of the priory started in 1618. George Preston of Holker Hall was the priory's benefactor, and he gave the canopies on top of the choir stalls and the oak screen.

The gatehouse is the only remaining monastic building, but it is believed that it would not have been the original gatehouse, which may have been close to the western end of the church. Over the years it has seen life as a guardhouse, a courtroom, and a grammar school. Beyond is Cavendish Street, where the main guest-house stood; this was to be converted into the Cavendish Arms of today.

Cartmel is also famous for Cartmel Races, a time when the village is crowded with people coming for the horse races held on the course close to the Square.

At the time of the Dissolution of the Monasteries, Cartmel Priory owned the land on which Holker Hall stands. This land was then annexed to the Duchy of Lancaster, later

transferred to the Bishopric of Chester, and subsequently sold to the Prestons around 1556. George Preston built the original hall in 1604. Since then, Holker has never been sold, but passed down through inheritance. In June 1697 Catherine Preston, having inherited the estate from her father, married Sir William Lowther, and Holker Hall remained with that family until 1756. Sir William's grandson, also William, died unmarried, leaving the estate to his cousin Lord George Cavendish, who was the second son of the third Duke of Devonshire, and it has been in the hands of the Cavendish family ever since.

Cark developed as a small industrial town at the time of the industrial revolution. The Engine Inn is a reminder of those times: it is named after one of James Watt's pumping engines, which was used to pump water from the tail race and back into the dam above the waterwheel. (However, Cartmel Priory owned its first corn mill many years earlier). The main cotton mill was owned by Messrs Thackeray & Stockdale, and operated for about thirty years from 1785. One engine in the mill was so noisy that it was heard for miles around. Later, the mill stood empty for five years until it was purchased by Edward Hall, a local farmer and miller, and converted into a corn mill, powered by water. It remained in use until a major fire in 1935.

Rows of cottages were built in Cark to provide accommodation for the mill workers and their families. Also, bridges were built across the beck to provide access. Cark station was once very busy with goods traffic as well as with passengers. The Cavendish family were able to request that the express passenger trains stop there for themselves and their visitors on their way to London and elsewhere.

GRANGE-OVER-SANDS, *The Pier 1914* 67426

The sea used to come right up to the streets of Flookburgh before embankments were built in 1797 which reclaimed many acres of land from the high tides. Its name derives from the fluke, or plaice, caught out in Morecambe Bay. Besides being a centre for fishing, it was a market town; its first charter was granted by Edward I, but these Tuesday markets were transferred to Cartmel around the 17th century. A major fire fanned by a dry wind burned down most of the town in the same century. Flookburgh is still a fishing village.

Kents Bank's main claim to fame is that it is the point of arrival of Cross Bay walks. The original Abbot Hall was where the abbot of Furness Abbey stayed when crossing the sands from Ulverston on his way to the abbey's Yorkshire estates. Nearby is Guide's Farm, long the home of the Queen's Guide across the sands of Morecambe Bay, currently Cedric Robinson. The post of Guide dates back to at least 1501, when the Prior of Cartmel is recorded as having paid for the first official guide across Morecambe Bay. Most of the housing in Kents Bank is modern.

Allithwaite dates back to the Bronze Age; urns from before 2000 BC have been found on land in Church Road. Its name is thought to come from Old English words meaning 'clearing by the Holy Well', a well on Humphrey Head that was dedicated to St Agnes. It was in use as a spa in the 18th and 19th centuries. The old buildings of the village are constructed with limestone extracted from a local quarry. The priory formerly had a tithe barn here. Close to Allithwaite is Wraysholme Tower, a pele tower built by the Harrington family in the late 15th century. Its walls are said to be cemented with lime and bullocks' blood, appropriate materials for what is now a farm building.

Lindale lies on an old route from Kendal across to Cartmel. It is probable that the Romans occupied the conical Castlehead, a rock sticking out from a former moss, for imperial coins have been unearthed there. It was once known as Atterpile Castle. John Wilkinson, who became famous as an ironmaster, lived here.

Grange-over-Sands was originally in the chapelry of Broughton East, although Cartmel is nearer. In Baines's 'Lancashire' of 1824 it is stated that James Bell of Grange was a victualler and guide over the Sands. The main industry of the village was hoop making - four hoop makers are listed.

Sarah Anne Clarke, a visitor from Liverpool, came to Grange and was shocked to find that it had no church - the nearest churches were at Cartmel and at Lindale. She set about raising funds, and various residents joined her in the work; a Miss Newby gave part of her garden as the site for the church. Some monies were raised by publishing a small book, 'Sketches of Grange' (a facsimile of it can still be purchased). The foundation stone was laid by the then Earl of Burlington in 1852, and the building, then much smaller than it is today, was consecrated on 13 October 1853.

The first incumbent was the Rev Wilson Rigg, who arrived by coach across the bay. The vehicle sank in the sands, and he was nearly drowned. His luggage and the coach were later recovered near Holme Island. In 1858 the Rev H R Smith was appointed as vicar, and he remained for thirty years. He saw the growth of the small village into a tourist town, and it was his suggestion that it become known as Grange-over-Sands to distinguish it from Grange-in-Borrowdale.

Grange had a small port, which was used by the monks of Cartmel Priory - they also had a granary there. This port would only have been a small one. Its site is believed to have been near the Commodore Hotel, (which was originally the Bay Horse Inn, built in the 1820s). The building of the railway embankment cut off this creek from the sea. Close to where the present railway station stands was a spot known as Windy Harbour, perhaps another indication that the old port was nearby.

The Ulverstone & Lancaster railway came to Grange in 1857. At first the line was only single track, but there was space for the second line on the landward side, and it was laid in the 1860s. It was then that the goods shed, still standing, was built. The first station was just a wooden hut with no other provision to shelter passengers. In 1863, Edward Paley of Paley & Austin, the Lancaster architects responsible for much work in the area, was asked by the Furness Railway directors to draw up plans for a new station. (The Furness Railway Company had bought the Ulverstone & Lancaster Railway in 1862). These are the buildings that still stand today. A new approach road was built from the road to Holme Island.

Mr Paley also designed the Grange Hotel, which is in keeping with the station design. It looked down on Windy Harbour. Before the coming of the railway, there were two hotels, the Crown and the Commercial, now the Commodore. The hotels had horse-drawn omnibuses that met the trains and conveyed people to them.

Grange was gradually becoming a Victorian holiday resort. However, it was spoiled by one thing, the stagnant Grange Marsh, which was crossed by the old approach road to the station. At that time, most of the land was owned by Benjamin Hall of Yewbarrow Lodge; he leased it through John Brogden, one of the directors, to the Furness Railway Company. They then levelled the old station approach, dug out the ornamental pond, and landscaped the whole area. Also, at that time the promenade by the railway and overlooking the gardens was built.

Bayley Lane Pier was built by the Morecambe Bay Steamboat Co in 1875 to bring trippers across the bay from Morecambe, something not popular with the residents of Grange, who did not appreciate these Yorkshire mill workers. It was replaced by the larger Clare House Pier, which was built in the 1890s. The last steamer called at Grange in 1910. In its later days the pier became just a jetty, which gradually fell apart - now nothing remains. Boating at Grange continued up to the Second World War, but the silting of what was a shelving beach made this no longer possible.

People arriving in Grange came mainly by train. As a result, the drives of the Netherwood Hotel, the Cumbria Grand Hotel and Hazelwood Court are all aligned to the station, and not for people arriving on the bottom road coming from Lindale. This road was built through to Holme Island in 1862, running alongside the railway and then crossing it to the island. Previously, Holme Island was reached by crossing the sands at low tide from near the station. Now, most visitors come by car, but the railway is still important; many people use the line between Barrow, Ulverston and Carnforth.

More of the story of Grange and the area around it unfolds in the following pictures.

HOLKER, CARK AND FLOOKBURGH

HOLKER HALL *1894* 34107

Holker Hall is built on lands that were owned by Cartmel Priory prior to the Reformation. The original house was built in the 16th century. The extensive grounds host the Holker Garden Festival in June each year, now a major event in the gardening calendar, and are home to a herd of fallow deer.

HOLKER HALL
The Interior c1875
7899

Lord George Cavendish rebuilt the house in 1840 to a design by the then Earl of Burlington, later Duke of Devonshire; this design closely resembled the original building. A fire in 1871 destroyed the west wing with all its valuable pictures, books, and furnishings. The fragments of a marble pedestal were collected and later incorporated into the chimney-piece we can see on the left of this view of the Hall.

HOLKER, *The Village 1912* 64388

Holker is an estate village dominated by the Hall and its gatehouse (left), which is now free of ivy. A water fountain stands by the road junction just beyond the picture. Opposite it are the estate offices, and in the wall of the offices is a Victorian letter box.

CARK
The Post Office 1897
40517

The plate by the window to the left of the door (now a window) shows that this was also the telegraph office and money order office, and also the Post Office Savings Bank. The middle window has gifts and photographs for sale. The building, now a private residence, is on the road to Cartmel, and is nearly opposite the former Constabulary Station.

CARK, *The Village 1912* 64385

The board on the house on the left proclaims that the building belongs to W H Duckworth, cycle and motor engineer. He had cycles for hire. Londis, the grocers, now occupies the area of bushes to its right. Boys are playing on the bridge over the beck.

▶ **CARK**
Mill Close c1965
C27023

Former mill workers' houses, now modernised, line the beck. Low Row is to the left, the lowest of three similar rows; Middle Row had been demolished by the time of the picture. The bridge is one of a number built in the 19th century – previously, Cark had just one bridge over the beck.

◀ **CARK**
Station Road 1912
64386

We are looking from the bridge by the railway. The road is devoid of both people and traffic – is it early morning? The third house from the right, slightly lower than its neighbours, is now the post office. Otherwise, the scene is little changed today.

▲ **RAVENSTOWN** *1918* 68318

Ravenstown was built during the First World War as an estate for workers at a close by airship factory, and was originally known as Flookburgh West. Once the works had been constructed, the scheme was abandoned, and Vickers took over the houses. Girls play on the Green, which is now occupied by houses.

◄ **FLOOKBURGH**
The Village and the Cross 1912 64390

The cross of 1882 was erected on the site of an ancient market cross. It records the fact that Flookburgh was granted its first charter by Edward I in 1278; a second charter was granted by Henry IV in 1412. John Burrow is shown as the licensee on the board on the Hope and Anchor Inn (right). A porch replaces the steps to the entrance door today.

◄ FLOOKBURGH
The Village 1912
64391

Someone, perhaps Mr Gillam the grocer who owned the shop (left), is writing on the blackboard: lard was 6½d, sugar 2½d (one penny today) and 4d, with bacon at 8d, and cheese 9d and 10d. Next door, with the curved front, is the now rebuilt former Co-op.

◄ **FLOOKBURGH**
Market Street
1903 50096

The only traffic is a cart parked by a barn on the right of the road, its shafts up in the air (right). To its left is the Crown Hotel. The shop on the left was J Slater & Sons, a tailor's and draper's. The only person on the street is a girl holding a baby by the house opposite the barn.

◄ **FLOOKBURGH**
St John the Baptist's Church
1901 47056

This church opened in 1900, replacing St Mary's Church, which formerly stood in the centre of Flookburgh. There is no clock in the tower at this date; the clock was installed as a memorial to those of the parish who fell in the Second World War. A representation of a Morecambe Bay fluke, a fish, is on the weather vane.

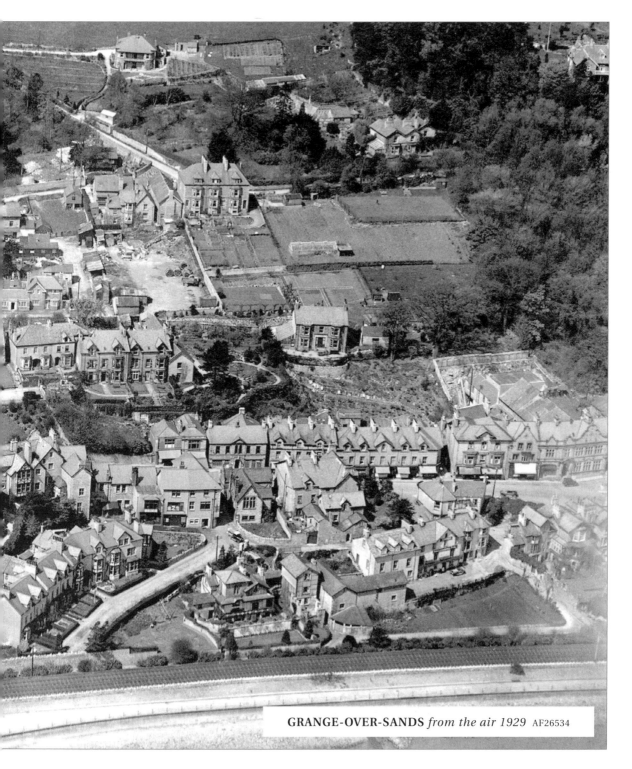

GRANGE-OVER-SANDS *from the air 1929* AF26534

ALLITHWAITE AND KENTS BANK

ALLITHWAITE, *Boarbank Hall c1955* A288027

On the 1851 Ordnance Survey map, this house is shown as Boar Bank Cottage. Then, it was owned by a wealthy lady, Miss Lambert; the building has since been much expanded to become both a Roman Catholic guest house and also a nursing home from 1954. The sixteen resident Augustinian sisters live in the building on the left, behind the Hall.

ALLITHWAITE
*Boarbank Hall, the Lounge
c1960* A288054

There are two virtually identical
lounges in the Hall, one at either
end. The main differences are
that this one has paintings on
the wall in panels on either side
of the fireplace and the other has
windows on both outer walls. The
paintings are beautifully executed,
and show birds and flowers in
their natural colours.

ALLITHWAITE, *Boarbank Hall, the Grotto c1955* A288022

A few metres into the woodland quite close to the Hall is this grotto. Fifty years from when this picture was taken, the
Madonna still smiles serenely in her niche to the right.

▼ **ALLITHWAITE,** *Lane End c1955* A288001

Many villages have a similarly named spot where lanes meet. The view was taken looking down Church Road from Cartmel Road by the crossroads, and is still much the same in appearance. To the left is Wart Barrow Lane, whilst the road to the right is Green Lane, which leads towards Boarbank Hall.

► **ALLITHWAITE**
Templand c1960
A288034

Templand is the farm to the upper right in this view, which was taken from Wart Barrow. Lane End is the crossroads in the centre of the picture. To the left, we can just see the church spire amongst the trees. Beyond is the Leven estuary entering Morecambe Bay.

◀ **ALLITHWAITE**
The Village 1953
A288028

Here, Allithwaite is decorated for the Coronation of 1953. This broader area by the village pub is The Square. Street lighting has not yet arrived here. The doorway where three men are looking at a dog has now been blocked up.

▶ **ALLITHWAITE**
From Jack Hill
c1955 A288012

Jack Hill drops steeply down to the farm at its foot. On that land, close to Humphrey Head, the last wolf in England is said to have been killed, supposedly by a member of the Harrington family. Boarbank Hall peeps through the trees to the top right.

ALLITHWAITE
The Village c1955
A288004

We can just see Boarbank
Hall above the trees at the
top centre of the picture.
Below, the white-painted
building would still be the
Royal Oak at the time of this
photograph; it is now the
Guide Over Sands pub. Jack
Hill is to the left - the road is
out of sight.

► **ALLITHWAITE**
Kirkhead Tower
c1965 A288003

It is thought that the first church in the district, predating Cartmel Priory, would have been on Kirkhead, giving the hill its name. The tower was erected as a summerhouse; it stands on private land owned by the Holker Estates.

◄ **KENTS BANK**
From the Sands 1894
34127

Note the signal box in the centre of the picture with the signals to its right. The cross sands route from Hest Bank and Arnside comes ashore by Kents Bank station, which is regularly used in summer by those groups of walkers who have been led across Morecambe Bay, wading the River Kent on the way.

▲ **KENTS BANK,** *Abbot Hall from the Park c1955* K147101

In 1840 a Mrs Carter died, leaving Abbot Hall, the second building on the site, to her wealthy niece, Miss Mary Lambert of Boarbank Hall. Abbot Hall was then rebuilt, and it was considerably extended in 1868, when the tower and south west wing were added. In 1915 it was purchased by the then Wesley Guild, and is now used for holidays and a conference centre.

◄ **KENTS BANK**
The Drawing Room,
Abbot Hall c1955
K147016

The drawing room of today is little altered in appearance from 1955 apart from new furniture, and is still used as a drawing room by the guests who stay here. One big change, however, is that a donkey does not go to the nearby railway station to collect their luggage any more.

ORDNANCE SURVEY MAP OF GRANGE-OVER-SANDS AND SURROUNDING AREAS 1848-1938

CARTMEL

CARTMEL, *The Village 1936* 82777

The display board to the right of the main shop window shows guide books and postcards of Cartmel Priory - the tree to the right is by the church. The newspaper placards tell of a champion jockey being injured, naval cuts, and a Scout Jamboree. Sun Maid Raisins were on sale from the machine above the seat by Bay Tree Café next to the shop.

CARTMEL
*The Priory Church
1894* 34096

The Priory Church of
St Mary and St Michael
was never elevated to
abbey status. The tower
has a unique formation:
the upper part is built
crosswise to the lower.
It is said that it is
theoretically unstable
architecturally, but it has
stood for 500 years.

CARTMEL, *The Beck 1894* 34104

A supply of fresh water was essential for the monks of Cartmel Priory, so they sited their monastery next to the very small
River Eea (pronounced Ay), which flows by the priory on its way to Cark and the sea.

CARTMEL, *The Church, the Harrington Monument c1875* 7895

The tomb is believed to commemorate John, the first Lord Harrington who died in 1347, and his wife Joan. It was not originally placed in this spot, but was moved sometime after the Dissolution. The move caused damage to the sedilia and piscina beside it in the sanctuary; other damage to the figures was caused by Cromwell's forces.

CARTMEL PRIORY, *Ancient Chairs 1912* 64378

In the 1860s, a grand chair was needed for a visit by the Bishop. In 1867 the then Duke of Devonshire gifted these two beautifully carved oak chairs from his seat at Hardwicke Hall in Derbyshire to Cartmel Priory ready for the occasion.

CARTMEL, *The Priory Gateway 1912* 64371

The gatehouse is the only remaining building from the priory's monastic days; the stone from the other monastic buildings was used in building the village. From 1624 to 1791 the gatehouse housed Cartmel school. It stands in the village square, and is now owned by the National Trust.

FIELD BROUGHTON, *St Peter's Church 1897* 40529

St Peter's was originally a chapel of ease to Cartmel Priory, and was consecrated by the Bishop of Chester on 30 June 1745. By 1880 the original building was in disrepair, and it was decided to replace it by the present church, which was designed by Paley & Austin of Lancaster. It is built of red sandstone in the Decorated style.

CARTMEL

From Hag Lane 1897 40525a

Cartmel lies in the bottom of a broad valley. It is said that this valley was once the outlet from Windermere, but it became blocked, so that the waters had to find a new course. Several paths descend the hillside to come out at or near the village, and one of these uses the stile over the dry stone wall in the foreground.

GRANGE-OVER-SANDS: THE PROMENADE

BEFORE the coming of the railway, the foreshore came right up to Grange itself; there was no promenade. The shore came close to various buildings, and the present wall round the ornamental gardens by the station is roughly the site of the sea wall.

The railway embankment as a whole was so long, covering eight miles of the tidal shoreline, that it had to be authorised by the Admiralty (Harbour) Department as a jetty. It was built by scraping sand from the beach, covering it with clay and then rubble, and then covering the whole with the limestone blocks which can still be seen in many places. Meathop quarry supplied most of the blocks. The seaward wall of the station itself was lapped by the tides.

In 1895 Mr Harold Pollitt, a director of a Helmshore textile factory, visited Grange; like many others, he fell for the town, and decided to make it his home. His generous help enabled Grange Urban District Council to start work on building the promenade, and Mr Pollitt established the tearooms close to the head of Clare House Pier. The pier had been built in 1893 by Richard Bush, and largely replaced Bayley Lane. Colonel Porritt, who lived in Yewbarrow Lodge wanted the promenade to run through to Kents Bank, but Grange did not want this – the townsfolk were afraid that Grange would develop on the lines of Morecambe or Blackpool.

THE PROMENADE TENNIS COURTS *1914* 67425

Tennis has long been a popular sport in Grange, and these courts are still in use today. However, the modern tennis players do not wear long trousers or skirts. Note the poles of the railway telegraph line behind the court.

THE SWIMMING POOL *1936* 87643

The swimming pool was finished in July 1932, but not officially opened until 18 August that year. That day, the key to the pool was handed to the Earl of Derby at the entrance gates by Lt Colonel Porritt. The Earl declared the pool open from the balcony, and after lunch, there were various swimming events.

THE PROMENADE *1929* 82783

The tearooms were built at the same time as the promenade; generous help was given to the Urban District Council for their construction by Harold Porritt. The swimming pool has not yet appeared.

▼ **FROM THE SANDS** *1906* 54222

The tearooms are to the left of the picture, with the bandstand to their right and Clare House Pier in the centre. This stretch of promenade was built between 1902 and 1904; the shed at the head of the pier was demolished.

► **THE PROMENADE**
1918 68384

The bandstand formerly stood on the promenade, but the ladies complained about its windswept position, which led to their having a dishevelled appearance. Also, they objected to being covered in smuts from the railway, which ran immediately behind it. The new site of the bandstand still remains close to Clare House Bridge (see 82781). This picture was taken from the bridge steps.

◄ THE RAILWAY
1929 82781

The ramp up to Clare House footbridge was built in 1903 - the date is inscribed in an elaborate brick date stone on its side. A Furness Railway locomotive from before the grouping in 1922 hauls a passenger train bound for Barrow-in-Furness. The bandstand has been moved to the park on the left.

► PLEASURE BOATS
1914 67426A

Many of the Morecambe Bay boats had names suggesting that they were bigger vessels, such as the 'Queen Mary' in the foreground -but she predated the Cunarder. She must have been very shallow-drafted to get right in to the shore with her passengers. Knobs at the stern and on the side by the mast suggest that she was also used for fishing and hauled a trawl.

THE MOTOR BOAT
1923 74147

The 'Silver Spray', an early
motor boat registered in
Grange, sets out with a
party of trippers, apparently
going towards Arnside. The
two typical Morecambe
Bay sailing boats have large
cockpits so as to take more
passengers on trips.

▼ **CLARE HOUSE PIER** *1896* 38513

The cabin at the top of Clare House pier still occupies its site; however, it was demolished when the promenade was constructed. Also, there is no ramp yet up to the bridge crossing the railway line and leading to Clare House Lane – it was built in 1904.

▶ **THE BEACH**
1912 64353

This scene is quite hard to recognise today, owing to the former swimming baths being on the right. Ahead, boats are setting off from Clare House Pier. There are now fewer trees to the left, where two very sombrely dressed ladies (mother and daughter?) are walking.

◀ **THE PROMENADE**
1921 70656

No longer do holidaymakers sit in folding deckchairs on the beach by Clare House Pier, which was then still being used by sailing craft. The tide still comes in, but across an area now covered by grass. Note the length of the lady's skirt (left) – summer fashions are much more revealing today.

▶ **THE BEACH** *1896*
38512

The anchor to the right would hold the boat in the foreground in place when the next tide came in. Behind it is Clare House Pier, with the end of the Congregational church visible by the trees. At the extreme right of the picture we can just see Bayley Lane Pier. Two boys are paddling in a pool left by the tide.

THE PIER *1914* 67426

This photograph, taken from the bridge at Clare House Pier, shows a busy scene, with eight boats of varying sizes gathered around. The two vessels in full sail have just discharged their passengers, who would not have long in Grange before having to return to Morecambe before the tide left the pier high and dry.

► **THE BEACH** *1912*
64347

A bare-footed
fisherman sits in his
boat at low water.
The board showing
the name 'Dewdrop'
at the stern suggests
that he also hired
it out. Fishermen
sometimes used to
take out adventurous
passengers to meet
the tidal bore coming
in, something that
would not be allowed
now for safety reasons.

◄ **THE PROMENADE**
1936 87641

Very little remains of
Clare House Pier. The
promenade is busy with
people, a number of
whom are partaking of
refreshments at tables
outside the tearooms.
Fashions have changed
considerably from
Victorian times.

▲ **THE BEACH** *1896* 38516

Paddling in streams and pools on the beach was popular in Victorian times. Note the hats and long dresses. There is no promenade yet, only the railway embankment; access to the beach was generally from a point near the station out of sight to the right.

◄ **FROM THE SANDS**
1906 54223

The original Crown Hotel stands to the left of St Paul's Church; the clock tower has not yet been built. In the centre, we can see Bailey Lane climbing steeply up towards Crown Hill, with the railway crossing keeper's house to its right at the bottom. Bailey Lane Pier has been demolished.

▶ **THE CROWN HOTEL**
From the Sands 1934
86183

The Crown Hotel stands
in isolation at the top of
Crown Hill, opposite the
Clock Tower. This building
dates from 1908, but much
of it was demolished
for the construction of
modern apartments; what
remained of the hotel was
incorporated into them.

◀ FROM THE BEACH
1901 47042

Neither the promenade nor the gardens by it have been built, and the stone facing of the railway embankment slopes right down to the beach. The Grange station starting signal is visible on the right. Immediately to its left is the Victoria Hall on Main Street.

THE PROMENADE
1914 67424

The large tree obscures
the original signal box. Its
more modern replacement
now obscures part of the
side of the shelter. There,
the stained glass windows
have today been replaced
with plain ones, and it has
been re-roofed without the
ornamentation. The railway
telegraph poles have gone.
Note that the two ladies are
carrying the then fashionable
umbrellas or parasols.

▶ **FROM BLAWITH POINT** *1898*
41045

The rocks at Blawith Point have not
changed in over a hundred years, but the
shore is now covered with grass. Grange
railway station fronts directly onto the
beach a third of the way along from the
right, for the promenade has not yet been
built. To its right is the former goods shed,
and peeping above the adjacent bushes is
the original signal box.

◀ **HOLME ISLAND** *1921*
70665

The original house on Holme Island was built by John Fitchett of Warrington in 1832. John Brogden of Furness Railway fame purchased it in 1851, and it was his son, Alexander, who enlarged the house and built the Temple of Vesta, which we can see through the trees.

GRANGE-OVER-SANDS: MAIN STREET AND THE ORNAMENTAL GARDENS

THE MANNEX DIRECTORY for 1851 shows very few businesses in Grange; all of them were included with Broughton. The six-inch Ordnance Survey map of the same date shows that many of the buildings on what is now Main Street had not yet been constructed. However, Bay Villa, on the side road down to the Commodore Hotel, is shown on the 1851 map; part of it dates back to 1820, and it was built on a site where there had been dwellings from 1716.

The map also shows a road through to Kents Bank, with Cart Lane and Carter Lane branching off from it, but no buildings have yet appeared there. The route to Lindale seems to have roughly followed the line of Windermere Road, entering Lindale above the church. The turnpike road of 1819 from Levens to Greenodd did not pass through Grange. It was not until 1875 that the road through to Lindale was finally opened.

Blawith Cottage, where the Netherwood Hotel now stands, was reached by a very minor track.

The Mannex Directory in 1866 shows a big change for the town. Grange is now listed separately from Broughton, and occupies half a page. A variety of businesses have appeared, including Mackerteth the chemist and wine merchant from Ulverston, who has opened a branch here. The town is referred to as a 'fashionable watering place'. Grange has started its expansion into the town we see today.

It is an astonishing fact that Grange nearly lost one of its main assets, the ornamental gardens. In 1892 it was necessary for the chairman of the council to use his casting vote to force through the purchase of the land from a Mr Coakes for £2500 so as to save it from developers, a decision that was not popular with many of the local people at the time.

MAIN STREET *c1960* G42138

This scene was taken from high up in the Crown Hotel, looking up the top section of Main Street. The windows on the right are in the side of the post office. The blind beyond juts from T D Smith, a grocer's shop, whose main store was in Lancaster. The library now occupies the field beyond.

MAIN STREET *c1960* G42125

On the left is the Palace Cinema, with the Palace Café above. It opened in 1922 and closed in 1963. Beyond, ascending the hill is Grange Fell Road; to its right is the field, formerly part of a piggery, where Beatrix Potter is said to have seen the original of Pigling Bland.

ST PAUL'S CHURCH *1906* 54228

No clock tower stands in front of the church as yet (see 67433 page 64). To the left is Borwick's Crown Hotel. This is the original building of 1789; it was so badly damaged by fire in 1908 that it had to be demolished. It was owned by the Borwick family - Mr Borwick lost all his clothes in the fire, and had to borrow replacements.

▶ **THE CLOCK TOWER** *1914*
67433

The clock tower was offered to the railway to be built by the station, but the offer was declined – so it was built by the parish church. It was presented to the town at mid-day on 4 December 1912 by Mrs Sophia Deardon, who was a local benefactor. Local limestone and St Bees sandstone were used in its construction.

◀ **MAIN STREET** *1906*
54230

The Lancaster Banking Company on the right was a forerunner of the District Bank, which became part of the National Westminster. Next door is R & H Law, cabinet makers and upholsterers, who also sold Nairns linoleum floor covering. Beyond them is Morris, a tobacconist.

▲ **MAIN STREET** *c1960* G42127

When we compare this photograph with 54230, we see that since 1906, R & H Law have expanded to occupy all the top four shops on the right, and had become a large furniture and upholstery shop. Following Law's closure, the top three shops became Lancaster's shoe shop, selling a wide range of shoes and boots; they are still trading there, but with an expanded range of goods.

◄ **MAIN STREET** *1891*
28638

There is no traffic on Main Street, which at this time had a problem caused by a dog-leg in the road by the tree visible in the centre background. Note all the blinds outside the shops on the left. The sign outside the shop on the right shows that they were the agent for Pullars, the dyers.

▼ **MAIN STREET AND THE INSTITUTE** *1894* 34118

The Institute was originally the local reading room, where people came to read books and newspapers. It was the first place of adult education in Grange. Now, it is used for various meetings and functions. Next door below is the agent for Pullars the dyers – they have crossed the street since photograph 28638, page 65 was taken. The only traffic is a horse and cart.

► **MAIN STREET** *c1955*
G42037

Sun blinds and signs jutting into the street are much in evidence. The old-style sign for Boots the chemists is in the centre of the left-hand row. J Trenouth occupies the first building on the left; the nearer part was then a tobacconist's, and the remainder of the shop a men's outfitter's. Now, the shop is just an outfitter's, but for both men and women.

◄ **MAIN STREET**
c1955 G42087

It is a busy day compared with G42037. Next to Boots, J Butler had a display of postcards. In the centre is a sign for K Shoes, then made in nearby Kendal. Postlethwaite's next door had a sign promoting the fact that they were painters and decorators and funeral directors.

► **VICTORIA HALL** *1901* 47051

The original title of this photograph as it appears in the Frith archive is 'Jubilee Hall'. This is most interesting, for the suggestion that the building be called Jubilee Hall in commemoration of Queen Victoria's Jubilee brought applause in 1897, when the council had the opportunity to purchase the land and remove the shop which was an obstruction in the road. However, it was finally named Victoria Hall, and the large building now houses various local societies' functions. The building also houses the tourism office, the police office, and the council offices.

MAIN STREET *1901*
47050

Between the right-hand blind and the entrance doorway was the London City and Midland Bank, forerunner of the Midland Bank, and now the police office. To the left of the tree a corner of the Commercial Hotel is visible; it is now the Commodore. The large tree has now gone, and the junction is much altered.

MAIN STREET *1912* 64360

The curved bow window to the right has gone, and the shop front is much changed; the building is part of the Victoria Hall, and the date 1898 appears at the top of the adjacent drainpipe. Next door, the building with the roof jutting out over the front is thirty years older. The bow windows have now gone; the one on the left in this photograph advertises china and glass, whilst the one on the right proclaimed that houses could be furnished for cash or on the hire purchase system.

FROM THE ORNAMENTAL GROUNDS *1901*
47047

This scene shows the view from near what is now the garden centre, and is somewhere near the site of the port of times past - the tide is now held back by the railway. The white-painted building above the left-hand end of the wall is the Commodore hotel of today.

THE ORNAMENTAL GARDENS *1891* 28637

In the centre a horse and cart stand by the pond; perhaps they have visited this spot so that the animal could have a drink of fresh water at Picklefoot Spring, which emerges here. This spring has a constant flow of water and a reputation for never running dry, even in times of severe drought.

▼ THE TERRACE AND THE ORNAMENTAL GROUNDS *1901* 47046

Yewbarrow Terrace, with its colonnades and cover for shoppers, had only recently been built at this time, but it still looks the same over 100 years later - even the rings to which to tie horses remain. The coping stones round the lake were put in place around 1900.

► THE LAKE *c1875* 7902

The artificial lake occupies land formerly lapped by the sea before the railway cut it off from the shore. The houses were then just above the shoreline. Neither Yewbarrow Terrace to the left nor the war memorial on the promontory on the right had been constructed at this date.

◄ THE ORNAMENTAL GROUNDS *1921*
70660

Coping stones now surround the edge of the lake, and the arch of roses that spanned Picklefoot Spring at the point where it emerges has been constructed. The shelter behind was constructed around 1900. Beyond, we can see Yewbarrow Lodge looking out over the tops of the trees and the park and over to Morecambe Bay beyond.

► YEWBARROW LODGE
c1970 ZZZ03431

Yewbarrow Lodge was the home of Lt Colonel Porritt in 1941, and it was also home to seven children who had been evacuated from Salford; ironically, the lodge was hit by incendiary bombs during an air raid. The grounds and Lodge were donated to Grange town in 1946. The house was closed up for many years whilst various schemes were proposed for it. In the late 1980s it was at last demolished to make way for sheltered housing for elderly residents.

THE ORNAMENTAL GARDENS *c1955* G42077

This photograph is quite similar to No 7902, page 70. The
buildings of 1875 still exist, but Yewbarrow Terrace has now
appeared on the left, and the war memorial on the promontory.
The dark tree to the right of the shops of Yewbarrow Terrace
is what is claimed to be the world's tallest decorated living
Christmas Tree. It is decorated with strings of lights each year.

THE GRANGE HOTEL AND THE TENNIS COURTS
1894 34116

The Grange Hotel was built following the coming of the railway. Its appearance was much the same in a town guide of 1961, when it was advertised as having central heating with fires in all rooms. By 1972 the fires had become electric fires, and the tennis courts had gone; now bungalows occupy their site.

AROUND GRANGE

KENTS BANK ROAD *1914* 67430

On the left is the village store, the Co-op, but with its original front. Beyond is the Methodist church, which opened as a Wesleyan chapel in 1874 on land given by Alexander Brogden; his wife laid the foundation stone.

KENTS BANK ROAD
1914 67429

At the left was Jackson's the butcher's, now an electrical shop. The sign below the fourth bow window from the left indicates a café – it is now a furniture store. The group of people are outside the then Congregational church. On the right is W Widgley & Co, a grocer's and confectioner's, with Entwistle the grocer's and baker's to their right. Now, the shops are a bookseller's and a hairdresser's.

THE PARK AND YEWBARROW CRAG *1936* 82787

The area known as Park Road Gardens was purchased by Grange Urban District Council from the Rev James Park in 1926. Shortly afterwards the bandstand was removed to this spot from its position on the promenade. It was refurbished and re-opened in July 1990. Close by is another small park on land donated by Dr Cox.

▶ THE CONGREGATIONAL CHURCH *c1955* G42045

The Lancashire Congregational Union founded the congregation in Grange in 1889. Six years later, this church, which has seating for 350 people, was opened; the buildings had cost £2400, of which half was raised by subscription. From 1972 it became part of the United Reformed Church.

▼ FROM ALLITHWAITE ROAD *1921* 70650

To the right of the bungalow on the left, which now has four dormer windows, is the roof of the Club Union Home, which was then topped with a small tower; this tower was demolished in the 1960s when the third floor was added. From 1990 it became Cartmel Grange, a private nursing home. A housing development has grown up in the field from which the picture was taken.

▶ THE CLUB UNION HOME *c1916* G42301

Before becoming a private nursing home, this building was a convalescent home for members of working men's clubs that were affiliated to the Club Union. Members needing to convalesce, usually for a fortnight, applied to their club's committee for a stay at the home. They generally took their wives, and the charge was normally met by the club. Often, this was known as the Miners' Home. It was erected in 1914 (the date appears above the stained glass main doorway in the centre of the building), and was officially opened in 1916. In the grounds is a stone statue of a First World War soldier, given by the Normanton Central Liberal Club - it can be seen from the road. This monument is now listed.

◄ FROM WOODHEAD
1894 34123

This photograph was taken from a spot near Westcliffe Gardens. The long wall is now broken for entrances to later housing. St Paul's Church, together with Holme Island, in the centre of the picture, are still to be seen from here.

▼ FROM GRANGE FELL ROAD *1921* 70649

We are now a hundred yards or so downhill from the place where No 34123, page 77, was taken. Highfield Road crosses to the right below the field. The trees behind St Paul's Church have gone today. Now, housing occupies the land on either side of the road, which leads from Grange to Cartmel.

▶ FROM CRAGG *1901*
47048

We are looking out over Grange to Morecambe Bay from Charney Well Road, which rises steeply above the town. Now, houses occupy the slope in front of the camera. On the left we can see the long, steeply pitched roof of the Methodist church on Kents Bank Road. Its neighbours had not then been built; the date stone on what is now McClure & Whitaker Ltd is for 1903.

◄ HAMPSFELL ROAD *1891* 28639

Two toddlers (left) are playing with a toy cart, something they could probably still do, as this steep road leading up to Hampsfell is little used by traffic. At the top are paths leading to Hampsfell Hospice, a viewpoint.

► THE HAZELWOOD HYDRO *1898* 41046

The Furness Railway Company once owned the Hazelwood Hydro. Originally it was known as Brown Robin Mansion, and was built as a private residence. It became a hydropathic hotel in 1887 following its enlargement. It was not licensed, and guests had to order their own drink a week in advance of their stay. This view shows the back of the building.

▶ **THE HAZELWOOD HYDRO** *1906* 54235

The Hydro looks out over marshy ground occupied by cattle of Grange Marsh Farm. In 1891 the residents could enjoy whist, concerts, dancing and games, and they played billiards. Did the Frith photographer stay here, and use their darkroom to produce his pictures?

◀ **THE GRAND HOTEL** *1927* 80485

The Hydro had become the Grand Hotel by this date, and it had been extended. It had also been known as the Golf Hotel - a golf course had been constructed on the land occupied by the cattle in No 54235. During the Second World War it was a training centre for RAF officers.

▲ **THE GOLF LINKS AND THE GRAND HOTEL** *1927* 80486

A game of golf takes place in front of what is now called the Cumbria Grand Hotel. Note the dress of golfers at that time – smart plus fours and thick socks. Since the course is on former marshland that was once lapped by the tides, it suffers from flooding from time to time.

◄ **HAZELWOOD TERRACE**
Lindale Road 1906
54231

The plaque in the centre of Hazelwood Terrace bears the date 1889. The house at the right has a sign for W A Tattersall, a coal merchant. The iron fence and bushes in the foreground at the junction with Meathop Road have now gone, and the old street lamp at its end has been replaced by a modern one by the side of the road. The terrace beyond is Berriedale Terrace.

THE CONVALESCENT HOME *1898* 41048

The North East Counties Convalescent Home for miners and other such workers would only recently have opened at this time, as only Phase One has been built; photograph No 47052 shows the completed building. It continued to be used as a convalescent home until it closed around 1958.

THE CONVALESCENT HOME *1901* 47052

Following its closure, the home lay derelict, and it was vandalised - even the ironwork at the top of the central section was removed. The grounds became a jungle. Locally, it was suggested that the building be demolished. However, it was taken over by the Stilling family in 1972, who have lovingly restored it and converted it into Hazelwood Court, a country house self-catering venue.

EGGERSLACK WOODS *1912* 64364

Eggerslack Cottage, which is tucked away in the woods, is one of the oldest buildings in Grange: it was built in 1841, predating the railway. The woods were formerly coppiced for making bobbins and other small wooden items, and are now home to a variety of wildlife.

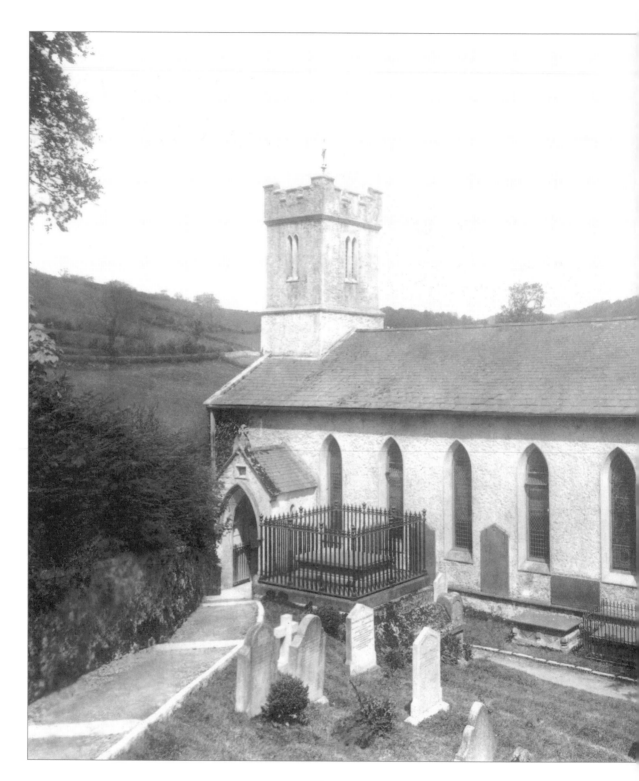

LINDALE IN CARTMEL

LINDALE IN CARTMEL
St Paul's Church 1898 41050

An ancient iron bloomery, or furnace, was discovered in
St Paul's churchyard in 1912 when the church was being
extended; this is very appropriate for the churchyard that
is the last resting place of John Wilkinson the ironmaster.

LINDALE IN CARTMEL
Town End c1960 L448014

The Shell garage is a reminder that Lindale has long being connected with motoring: traffic jams were common until the building of the bypass, and previously, Lindale Hill was notorious for serious accidents when all heavy traffic passed through the village. The Shell garage, Hadwins, is now much modernised. To its right is the Lindale Inn.

LINDALE IN CARTMEL
The John Wilkinson Memorial c1960 L448012

This pillar of solid iron in memory of John Wilkinson, the ironmaster,
was erected above the spot where he was originally buried at Castlehead
before new owners of the house had both him and his memorial removed.
Castlehead, his home, is built on a crag rising from what was a peat
moss before Wilkinson drained it. He tested the first iron-hulled boat
on the nearby River Winster. The memorial was removed and returned
after restoration work in 1984 by Dorothea Restoration Engineers Ltd.
The inscription reads: 'John Wilkinson Iron Master who died XIV July
MDCCCVIII aged LXXX years [14 July 1808 aged 80]. His different works
in various parts of the kingdom are lasting testimonies of his unceasing
labours. His life was spent in action for the benefit of man and, as he
presumed humbly to hope, to the glory of God'.

MEATHOP SANITORIUM *1901* 47053

Meathop Sanitorium was an isolation hospital for both men and
women with tuberculosis; its remote location was ideal for the
purpose. When they were well on the road to recovery, patients were
allowed to walk to a coal café for a cup of tea, which was served in
crockery kept especially for them.

INDEX

NAMES OF SUBSCRIBERS

The following people have kindly supported this book by subscribing to copies before publication.

Neil Ainsworth, Grange-over-Sands
Dr John & Hazel Allen, Cartmel
Jim & Pat Allison, Grange-over-Sands
Mr & Mrs Ardron, Flookburgh
Aunty Audrey from John & Ann
Sherry B & Andy E, Grange-over-Sands
T A Bailey-Pullen, In memory of Hazel
Our heaven, Arnie & Beryl Bain & daughters
Jim & Frances Banks & Family
Syd & Patricia Banks & Family
For Vera Banks, Robin & Sadie Simon
The Barrow Family
William Bateman
In memory of Marjorie Beecroft
K P & V P Benton
To recall local Grange historian, Eve Bernstein
Joan Bewley
Vikki Billington, Flookburgh
Mary & George Bird, Allithwaite
Jim & Freda Bradbury, Grange-over-Sands
To the Bradley Family from Neil
Mick & Ellen Bradshaw, Allithwaite
A D Briddock
The Brindle Family - 'Past, Present and Future'
Trevor Brockbank, Grange-over-Sands
Mr C R & Mrs A E Burns, Grange-over-Sands
Jennifer & Colin Burrow
B & A E Burton, Fell Road, Grange-over-Sands
In memory of Jane V Byrne
J P & P A Byrne, Grange-over-Sands
Maureen & Bob Chadwick, Grange-over-Sands
Ian & Julie Chambers, Grange-over-Sands
Mr W G D & Mrs M J Chappell
Gordon & Rosalind Clarke, Grange-over-Sands
In memory of Isabella Copeland, Grange
Mr & Mrs D Core, Grange-over-Sands
William J Cottam, Grange-over-Sands
Jean Cragg, Grange-over-Sands
Mr M J Crowe & Mrs P A Crowe, Grange-over-Sands
To Dorothy Culley with memories of Frank

The Culley Family, Grange-over-Sands
Victor Davies of Grange-over-Sands
Karen Dobson, Grange-over-Sands
Andrew & Gillian Dodd, who enjoy Grange today
Malcolm J Dodd, Ulverston
In memory of my mother Marjorie Drinkall
Ian S Drury, Templand, Grange-over-Sands
Mr E H & Mrs B M Edwards, Grange-over-Sands
Anthony & Jean Entwistle, Assco House
Mr & Mrs C Etherington
To Mrs G Evennett on her birthday
Mr J K Fawcitt, Grange-over-Sands
Sue Fleetwood
In memory of Bill & Mary Flunder
Noel & Jane Flunder, Grange-over-Sands
To Freddie, at rest in Grange-over Sands
In memory of my brave son Thomas Gleadow
In memory of Michael Goldsby
Paul & Helen Graham, married 1 May 2005
E W Green
In memory of Harry & Doris Greenhalgh
Margaret Grundy, Grange-over-Sands
The Guest Family, Cark-in-Cartmel
Mr & Mrs G Guy, Monks Rest, Grange-over-Sands
Tony Hall, The Library, Ulverston
In memory of Harry Hargreaves, Lytham
Mr JHLS Harrison, Grange-over-Sands
T R Hayward
Mrs M M Hobson, Grange-over-Sands
Helen Hodgkinson
Your heaven, Roy & Ruth Hodkinson & sons
David & Sylvia Holmes, Grange-over-Sands
Alec Hornby
Susan, Mark, Samuel & Benjamin Houghton
To Howard and Sally from Mum 03/05/2005
Jack & Margaret Howarth, Grange-over-Sands
Norman Howarth, 07 May 1929
Dr Ruth Hughes, Grange-over-Sands
Ian & Patricia Huitson, June 1991, Fell Rise
Miss G R Ingram, Grange-over-Sands

To celebrate the wedding of Miss G R Ingram &
   Mr J K Fawcitt 18th July 2005
Mary & Leon Jackson, Grange-over-Sands
Colin & Rhoda James, Allithwaite
Keith & Valerie James, Stott Park
In memory of Jim & Noelene Newman
To Jim, Merry Christmas, love Aunty Ann
The Jones Family
The Jopling Family, Grange-over-Sands
From Mum, In loving memory of C R G Kent
Mr D H & Mrs A Killian, Flookburgh
The Kings, Christian & Oliver, Cark Station
1905 Asplin-Lancaster, Grange-over-Sands
Alison & Andrew Leach 30/04/05
Shirley & Tony Leaver, Kents Bank
Dave & Ann Lenton, Grange-over-Sands
Dr & Mrs D Linklater, Cark-in-Cartmel
Ann & Ebony Lishman, Grange-over-Sands
Raymond Lishman, Oxenholme, Kendal
The Lisman Family, Grange-over-Sands
P M & E Lofthouse, Grange-over-Sands
Mr B & Mrs P M Miner, Grange-over-Sands
Trevor & Barbara Moore, Grange-over-Sands
Deborah & Kenny Moyle, Grange-over-Sands
To Mum from John & Ann
To Mum & Dad on your 55th Wedding Anniversary
   love Sue, Ian & Family
Susan & David Mycock of Thornleigh Hotel
Tom & Freda Newton, Grange-over- Sands
Ivor & Lotte Nichols, Grange-over-Sands
Grange Now
Mr A & Mrs J Oldcorn
Reverend W Alf Parker
Mark & Diane Peacock, Allithwaite
Dr & Mrs D C Pearson, Grange-over-Sands
Keith Pendrill RN, Risedale Home, Grange
Raymond Pepper, Arnside
D J & E E Phillips, Kents Bank
Peter & Barbara Ramsden, Grange-over-Sands
The Rawlinson Family, Grange-over-Sands

Nancy & Syd Rayner, Kents Bank, Grange-over-Sands
Chris Richardson, Wakefield
Pauline E & David B Richardson
In memory of Grandfather, Thomas Rigg of Grange
Mr P J & Mrs D Royston, Grange-over-Sands
Colin & Patricia Sharrock & Family
Dorothy & Ken Shepherd, Ulverston, Cumbria
David T Shepherd, Grange-over-Sands
Kevin & Terri Smith, Silver Wedding
Reverend N J Stancliff
Mr & Mrs N J Stott, Holker
Mr L & Mrs E Thompson, Grange-over-Sands
Memories of Thornber Grandparents, Burnley
Michael John Trenouth
In memory of Irvin Trohear, Kents Bank
Yvonne & Neil Turnbull
R G & M Tyson, Grange-over-Sands
Ann & Alec Waddicor
The Ward Family, Grange-over-Sands
The Wheatcroft Family, Grange-over-Sands
The Whiteman Family, Grange-over-Sands
Ralph & Anne Wilkinson, Kents Bank
Brian & Doris Winter, Grange-over-Sands
E M Wright, Grange-over-Sands
William H C Wycherley
Gordon Watts
To Sheila and Erwin Zirkel, love Sue, Ian and Family

FRITH PRODUCTS & SERVICES

Francis Frith would doubtless be pleased to know that the pioneering publishing venture he started in 1860 still continues today. Over a hundred and forty years later, The Francis Frith Collection continues in the same innovative tradition and is now one of the foremost publishers of vintage photographs in the world. Some of the current activities include:

Interior Decoration

Today Frith's photographs can be seen framed and as giant wall murals in thousands of pubs, restaurants, hotels, banks, retail stores and other public buildings throughout the country. In every case they enhance the unique local atmosphere of the places they depict and provide reminders of gentler days in an increasingly busy and frenetic world.

Product Promotions

Frith products are used by many major companies to promote the sales of their own products or to reinforce their own history and heritage. Frith promotions have been used by Hovis bread, Courage beers, Scots Porage Oats, Colman's mustard, Cadbury's foods, Mellow Birds coffee, Dunhill pipe tobacco, Guinness, and Bulmer's Cider.

Genealogy and Family History

As the interest in family history and roots grows world-wide, more and more people are turning to Frith's photographs of Great Britain for images of the towns, villages and streets where their ancestors lived; and, of course, photographs of the churches and chapels where their ancestors were christened, married and buried are an essential part of every genealogy tree and family album.

Frith Products

All Frith photographs are available Framed or just as Mounted Prints and Posters (size 23 x 16 inches). These may be ordered from the address below. From time to time other products - Address Books, Calendars, Table Mats, etc - are available.

The Internet

Already ninety thousand Frith photographs can be viewed and purchased on the internet through the Frith websites and a myriad of partner sites.

For more detailed information on Frith companies and products, look at these sites:

www.francisfrith.co.uk
www.francisfrith.com
(for North American visitors)

See the complete list of Frith Books at:

www.francisfrith.co.uk

This web site is regularly updated with the latest list of publications from The Francis Frith Collection. If you wish to buy books relating to another part of the country that your local bookshop does not stock, you may purchase on-line.

For further information, trade, or author enquiries please contact us at the address below:
The Francis Frith Collection, Frith's Barn, Teffont, Salisbury, Wiltshire, England SP3 5QP.
Tel: +44 (0)1722 716 376 Fax: +44 (0)1722 716 881   Email: sales@francisfrith.co.uk

See Frith books on the internet at www.francisfrith.co.uk

FREE PRINT OF YOUR CHOICE

Mounted Print
Overall size 14 x 11 inches (355 x 280mm)

Choose any Frith photograph in this book.
Simply complete the Voucher opposite and return it with your remittance for £2.25 (to cover postage and handling) and we will print the photograph of your choice in SEPIA (size 11 x 8 inches) and supply it in a cream mount with a burgundy rule line (overall size 14 x 11 inches).
Please note: photographs with a reference number starting with a "Z" are not Frith photographs and cannot be supplied under this offer.
Offer valid for delivery to one UK address only.

PLUS: Order additional Mounted Prints at HALF PRICE - £7.49 each (normally £14.99)
If you would like to order more Frith prints from this book, possibly as gifts for friends and family, you can buy them at half price (with no additional postage and handling costs).

PLUS: Have your Mounted Prints framed
For an extra £14.95 per print you can have your mounted print(s) framed in an elegant polished wood and gilt moulding, overall size 16 x 13 inches (no additional postage and handling required).

IMPORTANT!

These special prices are only available if you use this form to order . You must use the ORIGINAL VOUCHER on this page (no copies permitted). We can only despatch to one UK address. This offer cannot be combined with any other offer.

Send completed Voucher form to:
The Francis Frith Collection, Frith's Barn, Teffont, Salisbury, Wiltshire SP3 5QP

CHOOSE A PHOTOGRAPH FROM THIS BOOK

Voucher for **FREE** and Reduced Price Frith Prints

Please do not photocopy this voucher. Only the original is valid, so please fill it in, cut it out and return it to us with your order.

Picture ref no	Page no	Qty	Mounted @ £7.49	Framed + £14.95	Total Cost £
		1	Free of charge*	£	£
			£7.49	£	£
			£7.49	£	£
			£7.49	£	£
			£7.49	£	£
			£7.49	£	£

Please allow 28 days for delivery. Offer available to one UK address only

* Post & handling	£2.25	
Total Order Cost	£	

Title of this book . . . .

I enclose a cheque/postal order for £ . . . . made payable to 'The Francis Frith Collection'

OR please debit my Mastercard / Visa / Maestro / Amex card, details below

Card Number

Issue No (Maestro only)   Valid from (Maestro)

Expires   Signature

Name Mr/Mrs/Ms . . . .
Address . . . .
. . . .
. . . .
. . . . Postcode . . . .
Daytime Tel No . . . .
Email . . . .

ISBN 1-85937-801-3   Valid to 31/12/08

Free Print – see overleaf

Would you like to find out more about Francis Frith?

We have recently recruited some entertaining speakers who are happy to visit local groups, clubs and societies to give an illustrated talk documenting Frith's travels and photographs. If you are a member of such a group and are interested in hosting a presentation, we would love to hear from you.

Our speakers bring with them a small selection of our local town and county books, together with sample prints. They are happy to take orders. A small proportion of the order value is donated to the group who have hosted the presentation. The talks are therefore an excellent way of fundraising for small groups and societies.

Can you help us with information about any of the Frith photographs in this book?

We are gradually compiling an historical record for each of the photographs in the Frith archive. It is always fascinating to find out the names of the people shown in the pictures, as well as insights into the shops, buildings and other features depicted.

If you recognize anyone in the photographs in this book, or if you have information not already included in the author's caption, do let us know. We would love to hear from you, and will try to publish it in future books or articles.

Our production team

Frith books are produced by a small dedicated team at offices in the converted Grade II listed 18th-century barn at Teffont near Salisbury, illustrated above. Most have worked with the Frith Collection for many years. All have in common one quality: they have a passion for the Frith Collection. The team is constantly expanding, but currently includes:

Paul Baron, Jason Buck, John Buck, Ruth Butler, Heather Crisp, David Davies, Louis du Mont, Isobel Hall, Lucy Hart, Julian Hight, Peter Horne, James Kinnear, Karen Kinnear, Tina Leary, Stuart Login, Sue Molloy, Glenda Morgan, Wayne Morgan, Sarah Roberts, Kate Rotondetto, Dean Scource, Eliza Sackett, Terence Sackett, Sandra Sampson, Adrian Sanders, Sandra Sanger, Julia Skinner, Miles Smith, Lewis Taylor, Shelley Tolcher, Lorraine Tuck, Miranda Tunniclisse, David Turner, Amanita Wainwright and Ricky Williams.